SEEKING
YOUR
SPIRITUAL
IDENTITY

I0521838

LARRY CYRIL JENSEN
BRIDGER LEE JENSEN

SEEKING YOUR SPIRITUAL IDENTITY

Larry Cyril Jensen

Bridger Lee Jensen

WILL I TRAVEL
THROUGH TIME AND SPACE
FOREVER

Presented in this book are small gifts of poetry.

Beware, they will not give you a clear answer.

Possibly, each poem will leave you with a mystery.

Mysteries you alone will need to answer.

ISBN: 978-1-961677-24-1 (Paperback)
ISBN: 978-1-961677-26-5 (eBook)

Library of Congress Control Number: 2025925368

Printed in the United States of America

Published by:

info@thequippyquill.com
(302) 295-2278

PREFACE

This book comes to you through the combined efforts of a grandfather, father, and granddaughter. Its creation began as a set of poems, verses, rhymes, and sayings about spirituality and identity. But they all required interpretation, and it soon became obvious that the interpretations would not be the same for each reader.

The father and grandfather were originally fine with tolerating multiple interpretations, but the granddaughter, the child of the 21st century, presented an enhancement. The enhancement was to give the reader an explanation from artificial Intelligence.

The explication from artificial intelligence serves as a form of documentation of the message and thus is placed in a footnote following each poem. It is not considered to be the authors writing or material generated but an assist for the author to receive an independent explication of his work.

The fundamental goal and belief of the authors was that it is best, even critical, that each person should create their own interpretation. Accordingly, this book is organized to first present the poem or verse and page for each reader to record their own individual, unique interpretations for their life, spirit, and identity.

TABLE OF CONTENTS

PART I: IDENTITY

WHAT AM I

They say I'm a Spirit in a body.
But the evidence, the facts, they say
I am the only brain activity.
Me!
Just a circuit of electricity,
Something more I want to be. [1]

Explication of Poem by Artificial Intelligence

This short poem explores the tension between spiritual identity and scientific materialism. The speaker begins with the assertion they've heard from others— *"I'm a Spirit in a body"*—which reflects a traditional or metaphysical belief that human beings possess an immaterial essence. However, they contrast this with the "evidence" and "facts" they have encountered, which reduce their existence to "only brain activity" —a purely physical phenomenon governed by neural circuits and electricity.

By stating "Me!" in isolation, the speaker emphasizes their personal stake in the debate: their own identity and worth are on the line. The phrase "Just a circuit of electricity" expresses a kind of existential dissatisfaction with a strictly mechanistic view of life. The concluding line, "Something more I want to be," reveals a yearning for transcendence—an existence that surpasses the boundaries of biology and physical processes.

Ultimately, the poem is a concise meditation on the human struggle to reconcile scientific explanations of consciousness with the deeply felt desire for meaning, soul, or permanence. It raises questions about what it means to be "human" and whether our identities can—or should—be reduced to matter alone. Beneath its brevity, the piece holds a deep, universal longing to believe we are more than machines.

REFLECTIONS

After considering this poem, record your own feelings and thoughts about the verse.

_____

_____

_____

_____

_____

_____

_____

_____

_____

_____

_____

_____

_____

_____

WHAT HAPPENS WHEN MY BRAIN DIES

My brain will surely die
And then will I
Just disappear
And be nothing;
Not thinking, not existing
No awareness, no consciousness
Just darkness?
My intuition doth proclaim
Be a Spirit, not a brain. [2]

Explication of Poem by Artificial Intelligence

This poem wrestles with the ultimate question of mortality and the nature of self. The speaker begins with a stark acknowledgment: *"My brain will surely die."* This biological certainty prompts a deeper, existential inquiry—if the brain ceases to function, will the "I" vanish entirely? The imagery that follows — *"Not thinking, not existing / No awareness, no consciousness / Just darkness"*—portrays death from a strictly materialist perspective, where consciousness is extinguished alongside brain activity.

Yet, the poem takes a turn with the line *"My intuition doth proclaim / Be a Spirit, not a brain."* Here, the speaker's inner sense resists the purely physical conclusion. Intuition, often tied to deeper emotional or spiritual insight, asserts that the essence of the self is not bound to the brain. This closing declaration suggests hope for survival beyond physical death, envisioning the self as a spirit that transcends the body's end. The work reflects the human struggle between empirical evidence and personal conviction, between fear of oblivion and the longing for continuity. It questions whether consciousness is an emergent property of matter or an independent essence.

REFLECTIONS

After considering this poem, record your own feelings and thoughts about the verse.

_____

_____

_____

_____

_____

_____

_____

_____

_____

_____

_____

_____

_____

_____

I THINK THEREFORE I AM

Who or what does my thinking;
Does my brain think everything
Or does my Spirit say something?
Descarte said:
"I think therefore I am"
So is there a spirit in each man,
A spirit with intelligence and memory,
A spirit to make me be what I want to be? [3]

Explication of Poem by Artificial Intelligence

This poem reflects on the source of thought and identity, questioning whether thinking arises solely from the brain or from an immaterial spirit. The speaker invokes Descartes' famous statement, *"I think therefore I am,"* as a philosophical anchor, using it to explore the possibility that human existence is more than physical. The poem entertains the idea of a spirit—endowed with intelligence and memory—shaping identity and guiding desires.

By asking *"Does my Spirit say something?"* the speaker hints at an inner voice beyond biology, suggesting thought might be a collaboration between body and spirit. The tone is both curious and hopeful, leaning toward the belief that consciousness is not limited to brain function. Ultimately, the poem affirms a vision of the self as more than neurons—imbued with purpose, choice, and an enduring spiritual essence that defines who we are and who we can become.

REFLECTIONS

After considering this poem, record your own feelings and thoughts about the verse.

_____

_____

_____

_____

_____

_____

_____

_____

_____

_____

_____

_____

_____

_____

I AM WHAT I THINK I AM

It looks like I'm choosing just what I want to be
A Spirit in a body is the chosen me
Do I think just what I am?
Do I think therefore I am?
I do feel like a Spirit
Living in this place,
Expecting to travel
Forever,
Through time and space. [4]

Explication of Poem by Artificial Intelligence

This poem contemplates self-identity, free will, and the possibility of eternal existence. The speaker begins with a sense of agency—*"It looks like I'm choosing just what I want to be"*—framing identity as an intentional choice rather than something passively inherited. Defining themselves as "a Spirit in a body" aligns with a dualistic view: the body as temporary housing for a deeper, enduring essence.

The rhetorical questions—*"Do I think just what I am? / Do I think, therefore I am?"*—recall Descartes' famous declaration, but here the lines read as exploration rather than certainty. The speaker wonders whether thought alone defines existence or whether spirit transcends mere cognition.

The statement *"I do feel like a Spirit"* reveals an intuitive conviction that their truest self is not material. This culminates in the vision of "travel forever, through time and space," an image of limitless movement unbound by earthly constraints.

Ultimately, the poem blend's philosophy and hope. It examines whether identity is built by thought, chosen by will, or rooted in something eternal, while affirming a belief in the spirit's infinite journey beyond the confines of the physical world.

REFLECTIONS

After considering this poem, record your own feelings and thoughts about the verse.

_____

_____

_____

_____

_____

_____

_____

_____

_____

_____

_____

_____

_____

_____

FROM WHERE DO SPIRITS COME

My inner spirit
Must come from somewhere
Must then go somewhere.
Should I believe this?
Just...
Because I want this. [5]

Explication of Poem by Artificial Intelligence

This brief poem captures a moment of existential questioning, focusing on the origin and destiny of the spirit. The speaker begins with a quiet certainty—*"My inner spirit / Must come from somewhere"*—implying that their sense of self has a source beyond mere physical existence. This thought naturally leads to the idea that the spirit must also "go somewhere" after life, hinting at an ongoing journey or continuity beyond death.

However, the poem quickly pivots to self-scrutiny. The questions *"Should I believe this? / Just... / Because I want this"* introduce doubt, acknowledging the human tendency to believe comforting ideas without evidence. The ellipsis after "Just..." creates a pause that mirrors the hesitation in the speaker's mind, as if they are catching themselves in a moment of wishful thinking.

In its few lines, the poem distills the tension between hope and skepticism. It recognizes both the deep human longing for spiritual continuity and the intellectual caution against accepting beliefs solely because they feel good. By ending on this unresolved note, the work invites the reader to confront their own reasons for believing—or doubting—in the existence and destiny of the spirit.

REFLECTIONS

After considering this poem, record your own feelings and thoughts about the verse.

WHO IS TALKING WHEN WE TALK TO OURSELVES

We all talk to ourselves from time to time.
Who is speaking and who is answering?
One possibility appeals to my mind,
A brain and spirit communicating. [6]

Explication of Poem by Artificial Intelligence

This poem reflects on the familiar yet mysterious act of inner dialogue. The speaker begins with an observation most people can relate to—*"We all talk to ourselves from time to time"*—acknowledging the universal experience of self-conversation. The central question— *"Who is speaking and who is answering?"*—turns that ordinary act into a profound inquiry about the nature of consciousness.

The poem offers a possible explanation: that this internal exchange is not merely the brain thinking in loops, but rather a dialogue between two aspects of the self—a physical brain and a non-physical spirit. By suggesting *"A brain and spirit communicating,"* the speaker frames self-talk as evidence of duality, where cognition and intuition, matter and essence, are in active relationship.

Though brief, the poem carries a contemplative weight. It invites the reader to reconsider everyday thought as something potentially transcendent, a meeting point between biology and soul. The idea positions self-talk not as idle mental chatter, but as a subtle, ongoing conversation between our material and spiritual selves—an interaction that could reveal more about who we are than we might expect in our daily lives.

REFLECTIONS

After considering this poem, record your own feelings and thoughts about the verse.

_____

_____

_____

_____

_____

_____

_____

_____

_____

_____

_____

_____

_____

_____

PART II: WHAT MORE CAN I KNOW

A SIGN OF INTELLIGENCE

So much information I have been taught
But even more not taught.
Innate knowledge, feeling, and thinking
Is for me even more revealing. [7]

Explication of Poem by Artificial Intelligence

This poem examines the nature of intelligence, contrasting learned knowledge with innate understanding. The speaker begins by acknowledging the vast amount of information they have been taught, implying formal education or accumulated facts from external sources. Yet they quickly note that "even more" remains untaught—knowledge that cannot be fully captured in lessons or books.

The focus then shifts to "innate knowledge, feeling, and thinking," presenting intelligence as more than the sum of acquired data. Here, the speaker suggests that intuition, emotional awareness, and independent thought can be even more valuable than learned facts. This reflects a belief that true understanding comes from an internal wellspring, not solely from external instruction.

The poem's final line—*"Is for me even more revealing"*—underscores the speaker's conviction that inner insight often surpasses taught knowledge in guiding perception and self-awareness. Ultimately, the work portrays intelligence as a fusion of the learned and the inherent, with an emphasis on the deep, personal revelations that arise from within.

REFLECTIONS

After considering this poem, record your own feelings and thoughts about the verse.

CAN I EXPAND MY REALITY

Could it be:
There is something not sensory?
Could it be:
There is more I can learn spiritually?
Then hopefully,
I expand my reality. [8]

Explication of Poem by Artificial Intelligence

This poem explores the possibility of growth beyond the limits of sensory experience. The speaker begins with the repeated question, *"Could it be,"* inviting a sense of wonder and curiosity. The first possibility considered is *"something not sensory"*—realities or truths that cannot be detected through sight, sound, touch, taste, or smell. This opens the door to dimensions of existence that lie beyond the physical.

The second question shifts to the spiritual: *"Could it be: / There is more I can learn spiritually."* Here, the speaker suggests that spiritual learning—through reflection, intuition, or transcendent experience—might hold keys to greater understanding.

The closing hope, *"Then hopefully, / I expand my reality,"* conveys both aspiration and humility. The speaker acknowledges that expansion is not guaranteed, but possible through openness to what lies beyond the material world. Ultimately, the poem is a concise meditation on curiosity, spiritual growth, and the human longing to experience a broader, richer reality than what the senses alone can offer.

REFLECTIONS

After considering this poem, record your own feelings and thoughts about the verse.

_____

_____

_____

_____

_____

_____

_____

_____

_____

_____

_____

_____

_____

_____

ARE THERE TWO WORLDS

Impossible to ignore the world of logic and fact.
Eyes, ears, nose, taste, and touch keep us in contact.
But, is there another world our senses do not reveal?
An elusive world
To better think and feel? [9]

Explication of Poem by Artificial Intelligence

This poem reflects on the coexistence of two possible realms of experience—one grounded in sensory perception and another hidden beyond it. The speaker begins by affirming the undeniable reality of the material world, sustained by "logic and fact" and accessed through the five senses. This world is tangible, measurable, and in constant contact with us through our physical bodies.

Yet, the poem turns with the question: *"But, is there another world our senses do not reveal?"* This introduces the possibility of a parallel or deeper dimension—one that cannot be seen, heard, smelled, tasted, or touched. The description of it as "elusive" suggests it is subtle, perhaps spiritual or intuitive, requiring a different way of knowing.

The closing line—*"To better think and feel?"*—implies that this other world might enrich human understanding, expanding thought and deepening emotion. Ultimately, the poem is an inquiry into whether reality is solely physical or whether there exists an unseen realm that could enhance our mental and emotional lives, adding depth to both knowledge and experience.

REFLECTIONS

After considering this poem, record your own feelings and thoughts about the verse.

_____

_____

_____

_____

_____

_____

_____

_____

_____

_____

_____

_____

_____

_____

IS IT BETTER TO KNOW
MORE THAN LESS

Is there something in the universe
We can't measure with science and intellect?
Is there something else in the universe
We can only with our feelings detect?
I dare to believe this is correct.

Explication of Poem by Artificial Intelligence

This poem questions the limits of human knowledge, contrasting measurable scientific understanding with forms of awareness accessible only through feeling. The speaker begins with an open inquiry: *"Is there something in the universe / We can't measure with science and intellect?"* This frames science and rational thought as powerful yet potentially incomplete tools for comprehending reality.

The question is repeated with a shift—*"Is there something else in the universe / We can only with our feelings detect?"*—suggesting that emotion, intuition, or spiritual sensitivity might reveal truths that lie beyond empirical observation. This recognition positions feelings not as irrational distractions, but as valid instruments for perceiving aspects of existence inaccessible to reason alone.

The final line, *"I dare to believe this is correct,"* marks a personal leap of faith. The word "dare" conveys awareness of skepticism or potential criticism, yet the speaker embraces belief in a reality that transcends the purely measurable.

Ultimately, the poem is a meditation on epistemology—the nature of knowing—arguing for a more holistic approach that values both analytical reasoning and inner feeling. It affirms the courage required to trust non-scientific ways of knowing, suggesting that understanding the universe may require both head and heart.

REFLECTIONS

After considering this poem, record your own feelings and thoughts about the verse.

ARE WE SPIRITUALLY HARDWIRED

Tests now reveal so many kinds of intelligence,
Verbal, numerical, musical, just to name a few.
But finding and measuring spiritual intelligence,
Well, that's something new.
Clearly, some are born with more of it,
hardwired.
Still, for others, it seems to be socially acquired.
Fortunately, for many, spirituality will come
easily. [11]

Explication of Poem by Artificial Intelligence

This poem reflects on the concept of "spiritual intelligence" and its place alongside other recognized forms of human ability. The speaker notes that tests can now measure many types of intelligence—verbal, numerical, musical—yet spiritual intelligence remains elusive in both definition and measurement. By identifying it as "something new," the poem suggests that society is only beginning to explore spirituality as a dimension of human capability.

The idea that some people are "born with more of it, hardwired" frames spirituality as, at least in part, an innate trait—woven into the fabric of one's being. However, the poem balances this with the acknowledgment that for others, spirituality is "socially acquired," shaped by upbringing, culture, and life experiences.

The closing thought—*"So, for many, spirituality will come easily"*—carries an inclusive tone, suggesting that while the path may differ, the potential for spiritual understanding exists for all. Ultimately, the poem invites reflection on whether our capacity for spirituality is a product of biology, environment, or both, and whether recognizing it as a form of intelligence might deepen our understanding of human nature itself. It positions spirituality not as an abstract mystery, but as a real and varied dimension of human life.

REFLECTIONS

After considering this poem, record your own feelings and thoughts about the verse.

_____

_____

_____

_____

_____

_____

_____

_____

_____

_____

_____

_____

_____

_____

DO I KNOW THINGS NEVER BEEN TAUGHT?

Know something that has never been
taught?
Impossible, illogical!
But animals know things never taught
Why not us?
Our brains can create new perceptions
Our brains can create new inventions.
And could our spirits
Come with knowledge from an earlier time?
And could our spirits have
Another source of information?
Yes, yes, and
I do know that I now know
Things never been taught. [12]

Explication of Poem by Artificial Intelligence

This poem explores the possibility of possessing
knowledge that was never formally learned, blending
scientific curiosity with spiritual speculation. It begins

with the skeptical stance—*"Impossible, illogical!"*—reflecting the conventional belief that knowledge must be acquired through teaching or experience. Yet the speaker quickly challenges this, noting that animals seem to possess instinctive understanding without instruction. This opens the door to the idea that humans, too, might access information in unconventional ways.

The poem points to the brain's creative powers—its ability to generate "new perceptions" and "new inventions"—as evidence that not all knowing comes from direct teaching. From there, the speculation deepens: perhaps the spirit carries knowledge from "an earlier time," hinting at past lives, ancestral memory, or some form of preexistence. The closing affirmation—*"I do know that I now know / Things never been taught"*—turns the speculation into personal conviction. Ultimately, the poem celebrates the mystery of knowledge.

REFLECTIONS

After considering this poem, record your own feelings and thoughts about the verse.

_____

_____

_____

_____

_____

_____

_____

_____

_____

_____

_____

_____

_____

_____

IS ALL SHORT, NASTY, AND BRUTAL?

Said Thomas Hobbes in 1651
"Life is short, nasty, and brutal."
Yes, unfairness, tragedy to each will come.
At times, all will seem dark and futile.
But l look past today
Short will it be.
There is a better way in eternity
And as for today
Pleasant it can be. [13]

Explication of Poem by Artificial Intelligence

This poem responds to Thomas Hobbes' famous 1651 assertion that life is "short, nasty, and brutal," offering both acknowledgment of life's hardships and a hopeful counterpoint. The speaker concedes that unfairness and tragedy inevitably touch every life, and that there are moments when existence feels "dark and futile." This recognition grounds the poem in realism, honoring the truth of suffering without dismissing it.

However, the tone shifts as the speaker chooses to "look past today," reframing life's brevity as a gateway to something greater. The phrase *"There is a better way / In eternity"* suggests a spiritual or religious belief in an afterlife where the sorrows of the present are transcended. Eternity becomes a lens that makes temporal struggles appear small and temporary.

The final lines, *"And as for today / Pleasant it can be,"* encourage a balanced approach: holding hope for eternal joy while also seeking goodness in the present moment. This optimism does not deny hardship but insists on the possibility of beauty, gratitude, and meaning even within a flawed world.

Ultimately, the poem counters Hobbes' grim view with a perspective that blends realism, faith, and an intentional pursuit of present-day contentment.

REFLECTIONS

After considering this poem, record your own feelings and thoughts about the verse.

_____

_____

_____

_____

_____

_____

_____

_____

_____

_____

_____

_____

_____

_____

PART III: HOW TO TRAVEL FOREVER

MUST I TRAVEL FOREVER

Like it or not a trip I am taking.
A trip not of my own making,
Traveling wherever, going forever.
I may hate it or enjoy it.
I can't get off,
But if I accept it and direct it
I will forever be better off. [14]

Explication of Poem by Artificial Intelligence

This poem uses the metaphor of an unchosen journey to explore the nature of life—and possibly existence beyond it. The speaker acknowledges that they are on a "trip" not of their own making, suggesting that life's starting point and ultimate trajectory are outside their control. The travel is continuous—"going forever"—hinting at the idea of eternal existence, whether literal or symbolic.

The tone is pragmatic, admitting that this endless journey can be met with either resentment or enjoyment. The line *"I can't get off"* underscores the inevitability of life's forward motion, reinforcing the sense that stopping or escaping is not an option.

The pivotal shift comes with the conditional choice: *"But if I accept it and direct it / I will forever be better off."* Here, the poem offers agency—not in avoiding the journey, but in shaping one's attitude and actions along the way. Acceptance becomes a tool for empowerment, and direction a way to infuse purpose into the inevitable. Ultimately, the poem delivers a message of resilience: while we may not choose the fact of our journey, we can choose how we experience and influence it, turning inevitability into an opportunity for growth.

REFLECTIONS

After considering this poem, record your own feelings and thoughts about the verse.

_____

_____

_____

_____

_____

_____

_____

_____

_____

_____

_____

_____

_____

_____

FOREVER I MAY BE CHANGING

It is a very long trip I am taking.
Forever, I may be changing;
Growing through all eternity
And yes,
I relish the opportunity. [15]

Explication of Poem by Artificial Intelligence

This poem embraces the idea of perpetual transformation across an endless journey. The speaker describes life—or perhaps existence itself—as "a very long trip," immediately framing it as an ongoing voyage without a final destination. The repetition of *"Forever I may be traveling / Forever I may be changing"* links movement and change as inseparable, suggesting that growth is not a temporary phase but an eternal process.

The phrase *"Growing through all eternity"* elevates this journey beyond the physical realm, hinting at spiritual evolution that continues indefinitely. Here, change is not portrayed as loss or instability, but as expansion—an ever-unfolding opportunity to learn, adapt, and deepen.

The final declaration—*"And yes, / I relish the opportunity"*—is a bold embrace of this eternal metamorphosis. Rather than fearing endless change, the speaker welcomes it with enthusiasm, viewing transformation as a gift rather than a burden.

Ultimately, the poem offers a hopeful vision of existence as an infinite voyage of self-discovery and growth, where the constant motion of change is not something to endure, but something to celebrate. It affirms that openness to evolution may be the key to thriving in both time and eternity.

REFLECTIONS

After considering this poem, record your own feelings and thoughts about the verse.

_____

_____

_____

_____

_____

_____

_____

_____

_____

_____

_____

_____

_____

_____

DOES EARTH RESTRICT MY TRAVELING

Here on earth
We travel with restrictions;,
Restricted by where we live,
Restricted by when we live,
Restricted by body and mind,
Restricted by everything we find.
All these restrictions
Influence our destinations.
But then, it is our spirits
That overcome these limitations. [16]

Explication of Poem by Artificial Intelligence

This poem reflects on the limitations imposed by earthly existence while affirming the freedom of the spirit. The speaker begins with the straightforward truth that on earth, travel—both literal and metaphorical—is bound by restrictions. These constraints take many forms: geography (*"where we live"*), time (*"when we live"*), physical form (*"body and mind"*), and the circumstances we encounter (*"everything we find"*). Together, these boundaries shape and often limit the destinations we can reach.

However, the tone shifts in the final lines, where the spirit emerges as a transcendent force. Unlike the body, the spirit is not confined by space, time, or material conditions. This suggests that spiritual imagination, inner vision, or a deeper essence of self can break through barriers that the physical world enforces.

Ultimately, the poem contrasts the finite nature of earthly experience with the infinite potential of the spirit. While acknowledging that our journeys in this world are shaped and constrained by countless factors, it celebrates the idea that our inner, spiritual selves are free to explore beyond those limits—suggesting that true travel and growth happen within, unbound by the walls of reality.

REFLECTIONS

After considering this poem, record your own feelings and thoughts about the verse.

_____

_____

_____

_____

_____

_____

_____

_____

_____

_____

_____

_____

_____

_____

WHY FEAR DEATH

**So short this mortal living
And then we all fear leaving.
But why fear
To leave the nasty and brutal
To find the forever beautiful?** [17]

Explication of Poem by Artificial Intelligence

This poem questions the instinctive human fear of death, reframing it as a transition toward something better. The speaker begins by noting the brevity of "this mortal living," reminding us that life is fleeting for everyone. Despite this inevitability, people commonly fear "leaving," clinging to the familiar even when it is temporary.

The turning point comes with the challenge—*"But why fear"*—which shifts the perspective. Death is contrasted with life's "nasty and brutal" aspects, echoing Hobbes' grim view but placing it in a hopeful frame. Rather than viewing death as an end, the poem presents it as an entry into "the forever beautiful," a realm that is eternal and free from the suffering of the mortal world.

In its brevity, the poem carries both realism and optimism. It acknowledges life's hardships without despair and invites the reader to imagine death not as loss, but as a gateway to lasting beauty and peace—something to anticipate rather than dread.

REFLECTIONS

After considering this poem, record your own feelings and thoughts about the verse.

_____

_____

_____

_____

_____

_____

_____

_____

_____

_____

_____

_____

_____

WHO IS YOUR BEST TRAVELING COMPANION?

Whether you are traveling slowly
through eternity
Or
Whether you are traveling nearby
and quickly
Your best companion will be
Someone you can't see. [18]

Explication of Poem by Artificial Intelligence

This poem playfully yet thoughtfully considers the idea of an ideal traveling companion, whether the journey is vast and eternal or short and immediate. The speaker sets up two contrasting scenarios—traveling "slowly through eternity" or "nearby and quickly"—to show that the nature of the trip doesn't change the answer.

The conclusion, *"Your best companion will be / Someone you can't see,"* shifts the poem into a more mysterious and possibly spiritual realm. This unseen companion could be interpreted in several ways: a guiding spirit, an inner self, a divine presence, or even love and memory carried within. By leaving the identity undefined, the poem invites readers to project their own beliefs and experiences into the image.

Ultimately, the work blends simplicity with depth. It reminds us that the most meaningful guidance and support on life's journey may come from the invisible—forces, connections, and presences that accompany us regardless of distance or time.

REFLECTIONS

After considering this poem, record your own feelings and thoughts about the verse.

_____

_____

_____

_____

_____

_____

_____

_____

_____

_____

_____

_____

_____

WHY LOVE GOD

God hath said He will travel with me
through eternity,
He asks only that I love Him, heart, mind,
and soul.
But why does He need my love?
Why does He even want my love?
This I wanted to know!
Time has now passed, and I have an answer
at last.
It is that loving God is the sure way to grow
spiritually.
Thus, I must now to God confess
apologetically,
"Your first and greatest commandment
Benefits me more than thee." [19]

Explication of Poem by Artificial Intelligence

This poem begins as a personal inquiry into the
nature of loving God. The speaker recalls God's promise
to "travel with me through eternity," a profound

assurance of companionship beyond mortal life. God's request is simple yet all-encompassing—that He be loved with "heart, mind and soul." This raises an honest question: *Why would God need or even want my love?*

The speaker admits to wrestling with this question over time. The eventual realization is that loving God is not for God's benefit, but for the believer's own growth. The act of love toward the divine becomes the "sure way to grow spiritually," fostering transformation in the one who gives it.

The closing confession — *"Your first and greatest commandment benefits me more than thee"*—is both humble and revelatory. It reframes divine commandments not as obligations serving God's ego, but as gifts designed for human flourishing. Ultimately, the poem offers a journey from questioning to understanding, portraying divine love as a path to personal spiritual expansion and deeper purpose.

REFLECTIONS

After considering this poem, record your own feelings and thoughts about the verse.

_____

_____

_____

_____

_____

_____

_____

_____

_____

_____

_____

_____

_____

_____

ABOUT PROFESSOR
LARRY CYRIL JENSEN

Professor Jensen was born in 1938 and grew up in Wyoming, Montana, and Colorado. He is married to Janet and is a father to 10 children, 33 grandchildren, and 3 great-grandchildren.

After graduating from Wheat Ridge High School in Colorado, he received a B.S. and M.S. Degrees from Brigham Young University and his Ph.D. degree from Michigan State University.

Professor Jensen has taught at the following universities:
1. Michigan State University
2. State University of New York at Potsdam
3. Brigham Young University at Provo
4. Brigham Young University at Hawaii
5. Utah State University
6. Southern Virginia University

He has consulted for:
1. Research for Better Schools
2. Journal of Child Development
3. Psychological Reports and Perceptual Motor Skills
4. Family Research Center, Brigham Young University

5. Provo and Salt Lake City Public Schools
6. Institute for Population Studies in Exeter, England

His books include the following:
1. What's Right What's Wrong
2. Understanding and Using Social Influence Techniques
3. That's Not Fair
4. Moral Reasoning: A Philosophical and Psychological Integration
5. Responsibility and Morality
6. Feelings: Helping Children Understand Emotions
7. History of Moral Education
8. Stepping Into Step-Parenting
9. Adolescence
10. Parenting: An Applied Textbook
11. Family Feminism
12. Families: The Key to a Prosperous and Compassionate Society in the 21st Century

He has published multiple scholarly articles in the following journals:
1. Psychological Reports
2. Utah Personnel and Guidance Association Research Bulletin
3. Proceedings of the American Educational Research Association
4. Journal of Educational Psychology
5. Developmental Psychology

6. Journal of Experimental Psychology
7. Journal of Genetic Psychology
8. British Journal of Social and Clinical Psychology
9. Journal of Moral Education
10. Education
11. Educational and Psychological Measurement
12. Psychology in the Schools
13. Sex Roles
14. Journal of Psychology
15. Adolescence
16. International Journal of Social Psychiatry
17. Youth and Society
18. Journal for the Scientific Study of Religion
19. Journal of Business Ethics
20. Family Perspectives
21. Journal of Personality Assessment
22. American Educational Research Journal
23. Addictive Behaviors
24. Journal of Cross-Cultural Psychology
25. Journal of Research and Development in Education
26. Family Therapy
27. Religion and Public Education
28. The Family in America